JOE
DIMAGGIO

BASEBALL LEGENDS

JOE DiMAGGIO

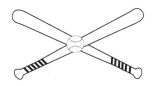

Marty Appel

Introduction by
Jim Murray

Senior Consultant
Earl Weaver

CHELSEA HOUSE PUBLISHERS
New York • Philadelphia

Produced by James Charlton Associates
New York, New York.

Designed by Hudson Studio
Ossining, New York.

Typesetting by LinoGraphics
New York, New York.

Picture research by Debra Hershkowitz

3 5 7 9 8 6 4 2

Library of Congress Cataloging-in-Publication Data

Appel, Martin.
      Joe DiMaggio / Marty Appel.
          p. cm.—(Baseball Legends)
      Includes bibliographical references.
      Summary: A biography of the baseball legend who hit safely in
fifty-six games during the 1941 season.
          ISBN 0-7910-1183-6
              0-7910-1198-4 (pbk.)
      1. DiMaggio, Joe, 1914– —Juvenile literature. 2. Baseball
players—United States—Biography—Juvenile literature.
[1. DiMaggio, Joe, 1914–   . 2. Baseball players.] I. Title. II. Series.
GV865.D5A85 1990
92—dc20
[796.357'092]
[B]

CONTENTS

WHAT MAKES A STAR

Jim Murray

No one has ever been able to explain to me the mysterious alchemy that makes one man a .350 hitter and another player, more or less identical in physical makeup, hard put to hit .200. You look at an Al Kaline, who played with the Detroit Tigers from 1953 to 1974. He was pale, stringy, almost poetic-looking. He always seemed to be struggling against a bad case of mononucleosis. But with a bat in his hands, he was King Kong. During his career, he hit 399 home runs, rapped out 3,007 hits, and compiled a .297 batting average.

Form isn't the reason. The first time anybody saw Roberto Clemente step into the batter's box for the Pittsburgh Pirates, the best guess was that Clemente would be back in Double A ball in a week. He had one foot in the bucket and held his bat at an awkward angle—he looked as though he couldn't hit an outside pitch. A lot of other ballplayers may have had a better-looking stance. Yet they never led the National League in hitting in four different years, the way Clemente did.

Not every ballplayer is born with the ability to hit a curveball. Nor is exceptional hand-eye coordination the key to heavy hitting. Big-league locker rooms are filled with players who have all the attributes, save one: discipline. Every baseball man can tell you a story about a pitcher who throws a ball faster than anyone has ever seen but who has no control on or *off* the field.

The Hall of Fame is full of people who transformed themselves into great ballplayers by working at the sport, by studying the game, and making sacrifices. They're overachievers—and winners. If you want to find them, just watch the World Series. Or simply read about New York Yankee great Lou Gehrig; Ted Williams, "the Splendid Splinter" of the Boston Red Sox; or the Dodgers' strikeout king Sandy Koufax.

A pitcher *should* be able to win a lot of ballgames with a 98-miles-per-hour fastball. But what about the pitcher who wins 20 games a year with a fastball so slow that you can catch it with your teeth? Bob Feller of the Cleveland Indians got into the Hall of Fame with a blazing fastball that glowed in the dark. National League star Grover Cleveland Alexander got there with a pitch that took considerably longer to reach the plate; but when it did arrive, the pitch was exactly where Alexander wanted it to be— and the last place the batter expected it to be.

There are probably more players with exceptional ability who didn't make it to the major leagues than there are who did. A number of great hitters, bored with fielding practice, had to be dropped from their team because their home-run production didn't make up for their lapses in the field. And then there are players like Brooks Robinson of the Baltimore Orioles, who made himself into a human vacuum cleaner at third base because he knew that working hard to become an expert fielder would win him a job in the big leagues.

A star is not something that flashes through the sky. That's a comet. Or a meteor. A star is something you can steer ships by. It stays in place and gives off a steady glow; it is fixed, permanent. A star works at being a star.

And that's how you tell a star in baseball. He shows up night after night and takes pride in how brightly he shines. He's Willie Mays running so hard his hat keeps falling off; Ty Cobb sliding to stretch a single into a double; Lou Gehrig, after being fooled in his first two at-bats, belting the next pitch off the light tower because he's taken the time to study the pitcher. Stars never take themselves for granted. That's why they're stars.

1
A HEROIC RETURN

In the late 1940s, the New York Yankees and Boston Red Sox were two outstanding ballclubs. Since both cities were on the East Coast, the competition between them was intense. Whenever they played each other, whether at charming little Fenway Park in Boston, or New York's magnificent and historic Yankee Stadium, baseball interest was enormous. The fact that two of the best players of the day—Boston's Ted Williams and New York's Joe DiMaggio—were then at the peaks of their careers, only made the competition better.

The rivalry in 1949 was especially great because the Yankees had a new manager—Casey Stengel—while the Red Sox were being managed by Joe McCarthy, who had formerly led New York to so many great seasons. But late in June, as the two teams prepared to meet in Fenway Park for the biggest series of the season, Yankee fans were less than confident. The big question was: Would DiMaggio be playing?

Joe DiMaggio was not enjoying one of his best years. A bone spur in his right foot had him limping around on crutches instead of playing center field for the Yanks. He had yet to appear in his first game of the season, and many people thought his career might be over. Even DiMaggio himself, who was always sure of his own abilities, must have wondered how he could possibly drop into the lineup in midseason, with no training period, and perform at his best.

As the Yankees traveled to Boston, DiMaggio's return still seemed doubtful. But he took some batting practice anyway, then told Stengel he was ready to play. For the first time as Yankee manager, Stengel was able to insert DiMaggio's name into the starting lineup. He didn't really expect much from Joe, but he hoped that his mere presence would give a big boost to the other Yankees. They had great respect for him—and with good reason!

In his first game back, DiMaggio did everything his teammates could have asked. He singled, homered, broke up a double play with a hard slide, and caught the final deep fly ball off Ted Williams's bat for a Yankee victory.

The next day, with the Yankees losing 7–1, he hit a three-run homer to make it 7–4. And when the Yankees tied it up at 7–7, DiMaggio homered again to win it 9–7.

On the third day of the series, DiMaggio homered yet again to help clinch a series sweep. Four home runs plus a single in eleven times at bat, with nine runs batted in!

DiMaggio's sensational return to the Yankee lineup, under the most competitive pressure, was the talk of the nation. Even people who didn't follow baseball spoke in awe of "the Great DiMaggio's" feats. And even today, people who saw him then claim that no one has ever come along who could play the game to such perfection.

DiMaggio played in an era before television;

more people watch a single World Series game today on TV than saw DiMaggio in person throughout his entire career. But one only had to hear of his exploits, to listen to his teammates and his managers, to understand what a special athlete he was.

That DiMaggio became a baseball player at all was a matter of good fortune, for unlike most of today's athletes, he was a "first generation" baseball player. His parents were hard-working immigrants who knew nothing of the game and had no time to teach it to their children. But in just a few years, Joe not only learned the game but became one of the true sports heroes of his time.

2

THE SON OF A FISHERMAN

Joe's parents, Rosalie and Giuseppe Paolo DiMaggio, were born on the island of Sicily in southern Italy. Giuseppe worked as a fisherman there until 1898, when his father-in-law, who was already in America, sent for him. As soon as he was settled in the San Francisco area, Giuseppe started job hunting, but the only work he could find was as a railroad laborer earning ten cents an hour. It took him four years to save enough money to bring his wife and daughter over from Italy.

In the years that followed, the DiMaggios had seven more children. Joseph Paul DiMaggio, the sixth of those seven, was born on November 25, 1914, in Martinez, California. Giuseppe Paolo was "Joseph Paul" in English, and young Joe was named after his father. When Joe was less than a year old, the family moved to a four-room house on Taylor Street in the North Beach section of San Francisco. By then, Giuseppe had found a job fishing, but money was still scarce. With eight children to clothe and feed, the family struggled to make ends meet.

There were five boys in all: Tom, Michael, and

Joe at age three, in the DiMaggios' backyard in San Francisco, California.

The DiMaggio brothers— Joe, Vince, and Dom—get together for a reunion at San Francisco's Fisherman's Wharf in January 1946, after Joe and Dom returned from four years of military service.

Vince were born before Joe, and Dominic was born after. Giuseppe hoped they would all become fishermen, but the boys had their own plans for the future. Although the children spoke Italian to their parents, they used English with each other and in school. They were U.S. citizens, spoke without accents, and grew up with the "American dream" that you could become anything you wanted with a lot of hard work and a little bit of luck. And there were few things as American as the sport of baseball.

Certainly Joe's idea of the American dream did not include rising before dawn and setting out to sea each day. He suffered from severe seasickness, and he wasn't especially fond of the smell of fish either.

Joe made his way through the Hancock

Grammar School, Francisco Junior High School, and Galileo High School, but his interest in sports was much greater than his interest in schoolwork. When he was about ten years old, he began playing sandlot ball, using a cutoff boat oar for a bat and a wad of rolled-up tape for a baseball. None of the neighborhood kids could afford a glove, but they all loved the game. Their dirt field was called the "horse lot," because that was where the local dairy parked its milk wagons overnight.

3

JOE THE PRO

When Joe was a boy, there was no major-league baseball team in San Francisco. In fact there was no team farther west than St. Louis, and the only place a fan could see big stars like Babe Ruth and Ty Cobb was on movie house newsreels. Fortunately, the Pacific Coast League was a wonderful stronghold of talented players and exciting teams. In San Francisco alone, two teams—the Seals and the Missions—played high-caliber professional ball. While technically speaking this was minor-league baseball, it was played on a very high level, most of the cities in the league eventually did join the majors, and many of the players went on to greatness in the major leagues. Other equally talented players spent their whole careers in the PCL. Since there were only 16 major-league teams then, as opposed to 26 today, not many jobs were open, and a lot of worthy players never made it to the big leagues.

Lefty O'Doul was an example of one who did. O'Doul signed with the Seals as a pitcher in 1917 and later became an outfielder. With his .349 major-league career average, he became a legend in the PCL, batting as high as .392 one

DiMaggio at age 17 in the uniform of the San Francisco Seals.

season. He was a hero to most young San Francisco baseball fans, including the DiMaggio brothers.

Joe's father did not share his sons' love of baseball. He thought Joe was wasting his time with this game, and argued that he'd be better off fishing instead. Tom, the oldest brother, was a good athlete, but he followed his father's advice and turned down an offer to try out for the Seals.

In 1927, Joe entered the Boys Club League as a third baseman and shortstop. It was the first time he got to play with good equipment, and he won two gold-plated baseballs and sixteen dollars worth of merchandise from a local store when his team won the championship. That was a lot of money then, and it may have made Giuseppe take baseball a bit more seriously.

At Francisco Junior High, Joe weighed 130 pounds and was recognized as the school's best athlete. While he was especially good at tennis, baseball was his first love. He spent countless hours playing catch with his brothers Vince and Dominic.

To help his family, Joe took some odd jobs as a newsboy, a delivery boy, and a dock worker. But he was extremely shy and preferred to keep to himself—except for baseball games, of course.

In tenth grade, Joe decided to quit school. The year was 1931, and America was deep into the Great Depression. Millions of people were out of work and times were tough. Those who had once held high-paying jobs were now willing to do anything to make a dollar, whether it was selling apples on a street corner or sweeping railway stations. Before long, almost 15 million Americans would be unemployed out of some 53 million who were eligible to work. It was not a good time to hit the streets, and Joe's dad had some strong opinions on the matter. He knew even a young man with a good education would have a hard time finding decent employment. And a high school dropout, he warned his son, wouldn't stand a chance. But although Joe was always soft-spoken, he could be stubborn as well. When he was sure of what he wanted, there was no talking him out of it. And now he was sure. As was often the case, Joe's mother came to his defense, and his father reluctantly accepted his decision to leave school.

Joe signed up with an amateur team called Sunset Produce, and in 18 games he batted an amazing .632. One day when Sunset was playing against a "junior varsity" team affiliated with the Missions, Joe was spotted by the Missions' manager, Fred Hoffman. A former major leaguer, Hoffman knew talent when he saw it, and he offered Joe a tryout.

But Joe's brother Vince was already signed up to play with the rival Seals, and he told Joe not to sign too quickly. Vince spoke to Seals scout Spike Hennessy, who, legend has it, found Joe peering into Seals Stadium through a knothole in the outfield fence one day, trying to watch his brother play.

"Would you like to come in?" Hennessy is said to have suggested. When Joe said yes, he was surprised to be taken to the office of the team owner Charlie Graham rather than to the bleachers.

Charlie Graham did not ask Joe to try out. He was confident that the brother of Vince DiMaggio would be a good player too. Besides, though Joe was thin and angular, he was obviously strong, with the body of an athlete. Vince had told the Seals all about the Missions' interest in his brother, and that was good enough for Charlie Graham.

The Seals were a minor-league team not connected with any farm system. Like most minor-league owners, Graham ran the team mainly to sell tickets and occasionally to sell a player to a major-league club. Before the current farm system of player development was created, most players started out just that way.

The Pacific Coast League season was a long one—187 games compared to the major leagues' 154 game schedules. The PCL was made up of teams from Los Angeles, Hollywood, Oakland, San Diego, Portland, Sacramento, Seattle, and San Francisco. It would be the first opportunity

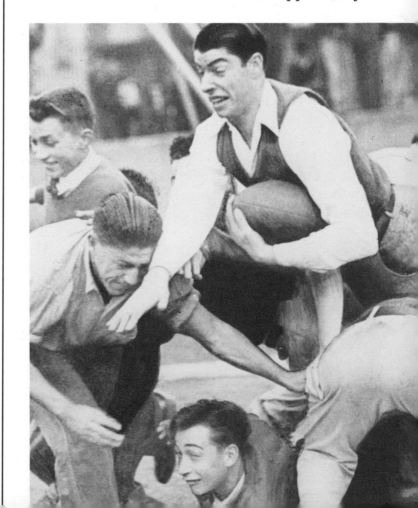

for the 18-year-old DiMaggio to travel away from home, stay in a hotel, and fend for himself. And with so many games to play, he'd have plenty of time to develop his great skills. Best of all, he'd be playing with his brother Vince again.

Joe happily accepted the Seals' offer. And this time even Giuseppe was impressed. He had two sons getting paid to play ball during the Depression. Although he never did learn to read English, Giuseppe became enough of a fan to turn to the sports page in the newspaper and find the name "DiMaggio" in the baseball stories.

Joe played the last three games of the 1932 season at shortstop for the Seals. His fielding was not much to brag about, but he hit a triple his first time at bat. To no one's surprise, he was

DiMaggio carries the ball during a 1933 pickup football game with his buddies in San Francisco.

offered a full season's contract for 1933. He would receive $225 a month, about $100 more than most rookies received. Obviously, the Seals felt they had a great talent signed up.

Despite the big contract, Joe began the year on the bench. But then his brother Vince developed a sore arm, and Joe was sent out to replace him in right field. That marked the end of his days as an infielder, and the beginning of his days as a star. Within a matter of weeks, Joe DiMaggio was the talk of San Francisco, and it wouldn't be long before he was known all over the world.

Joe's fame really began to spread on May 28, 1933, the second month of his official rookie season, when he began a sensational 61-game hitting streak. The streak finally ended July 25, but by then DiMaggio had made his mark. The mayor of San Francisco presented him with a watch to celebrate the great feat; and with his picture in the newspaper nearly every day, Joe was recognized all over town. It was not the longest batting streak in minor-league history (in 1919 a Western Association player named Joe Wilhoit had batted safely in 69 straight games), but no one had ever done anything like this against such tough competition.

When Vince was traded to Hollywood, Joe stayed on in right field. He quickly proved himself an outfielder of confidence and ability. Throwing out runners with great regularity, he led the league with 32 assists. At the plate, Joe was even more impressive, racking up a season's batting average of .340 with 28 home runs and 169 runs batted in, tops in the league. He had 259 hits.

Joe started off the 1934 season just as impressively. By July he already had 12 homers

On July 13, 1933, the 18-year-old DiMaggio tied the Pacific Coast League record with a 49-game hitting streak. This home run was one of three hits he got that day. The streak was finally stopped at 61.

and a .341 average. But then a freak accident almost ended his career. Riding home in a cab after visiting with his sister, Joe felt his foot fall asleep. As he got up to leave the cab, he put his weight on the leg and dropped to the ground in pain.

At a nearby hospital, he was treated with hot towels and salt packs and then sent home. But when his knee gave out under him the next morning, DiMaggio realized that this was no ordinary injury.

Doctors put his entire leg in a splint for three weeks and he was through for the year.

For a while it looked as though DiMaggio might be through forever—at least as far as the big leagues were concerned. Everyone in the majors had been scouting him since his sensational hitting streak. He already figured to be the highest-paid minor leaguer ever to come along. But now, as scouts looked at the leg in an aluminum splint, almost all interest disappeared. The only club that didn't write DiMaggio off was the New York Yankees, DiMaggio's favorite team.

4

THE YANKEES TAKE A CHANCE

The Yankees had two West Coast scouts, Bill Essick and Joe Devine, who had been watching DiMaggio for quite a while. Essick could not believe that a 19-year-old with such outstanding ability would be stopped by a bad knee. He urged Charlie Graham to have DiMaggio examined in Los Angeles. When the doctor's report was optimistic, the Yankees offered the Seals $25,000 plus five players for DiMaggio. Graham accepted, and the Yankees had themselves a ballplayer, bad knee and all.

DiMaggio didn't move up to New York immediately. Although they now owned his contract, the Yanks agreed to let him play one more year in San Francisco. Charlie Graham was as happy as could be, for DiMaggio was the hottest attraction in town. And it soon became clear that the Yankees hadn't become baseball's most successful team by accident. While everyone else had closed their wallets as soon as DiMaggio developed the trick knee, the Yankees were willing to take a chance on him. And in 1935, DiMaggio made their gamble pay off. He returned to bat a sensational .398 for the Seals

Wrapped in a blanket to warm him against the chilly New York spring, DiMaggio accommodates young fans with an autograph.

with 34 home runs and 154 RBI's. Then, after winning the Most Valuable Player Award, he said goodbye forever to the minor leagues and headed for the big time.

At 21 years of age, DiMaggio set out for his first major-league spring training camp with two veteran Yankees from San Francisco, Tony Lazzeri and Frank Crosetti. Although they had agreed to drive to Florida together, DiMaggio had failed to mention one important fact: he didn't know how to drive! It was a long, silent 3,000-mile journey for the new young Yank.

The Yankees of 1936, managed by Joe McCarthy, had not been in a World Series since 1932. For most teams, that would be no cause for concern. But the Yankees weren't just any team. Ever since 1921 they had been baseball's most successful team. Led by superstar Babe Ruth, they'd won seven pennants, setting new attendance records wherever they played.

After Ruth played his last season for the Yankees in 1934, Lou Gehrig, the team's mighty first baseman, did his best to keep the Yankees on the top. But he couldn't do it alone. A tremendous player, Gehrig had spent his entire career playing in Ruth's shadow. But now, with Ruth gone, the team seemed to need someone else to join Gehrig in the middle of the lineup. And many fans and experts thought Joe DiMaggio just might be the one. DiMaggio was the most eagerly awaited rookie since the Cardinals had signed the flashy Dizzy Dean in 1930. But flashy was what DiMaggio wasn't. He was still very shy, and had little to say to the New York sportswriters who were interested in his every move—both on and off the field.

Although DiMaggio did not have Dean's humor, or Ruth's charisma, he did have the kind

of quiet dignity that McCarthy liked. During the Ruth years, the Yankees had been known as a fun-loving, hard-living team. But now McCarthy wanted to mold the team more into Gehrig's image—strong and silent, with heads held high. DiMaggio seemed to fit that ideal naturally, as did catcher Bill Dickey. But luckily for DiMaggio there was still the light-hearted pitcher Lefty Gomez around to relax the guys and remind everyone that baseball could be fun too.

Gomez was a big help to DiMaggio as the young rookie discovered New York for the first time and adjusted to life in the nation's biggest city. Once Gomez questioned DiMaggio's determination to play a shallow center field, much in the style of Tris Speaker, a great center fielder from the 1910's and 1920's. "Don't worry," said DiMaggio, "I can cover the ground. I'll make the fans forget Tris Speaker."

Gomez answered, "I'm worried that you'll make them forget Lefty Gomez!"

In 1936, Tony Lazzeri (left), Joe DiMaggio, and Frank Crosetti drove all the way from California to Florida for DiMaggio's first Yankee spring training camp. This photo shows the three teammates during an early workout.

Joe DiMaggio may have been a man of few words, but that was okay. His bat spoke for him! The newspapers were full of his spring training exploits. But just as the team was preparing to wind up camp and head north, DiMaggio hurt his left ankle and needed diathermy, or heat lamp, treatments to heal it. Unfortunately, too much heat was applied and DiMaggio developed a burn that was severe enough to keep him on the bench until May 5.

DiMaggio celebrated his long-overdue debut with a sixth-inning triple. Wearing uniform #9 (he later switched to #5), DiMaggio played left field that day. But shortly thereafter, the Yankees traded their center fielder, Ben Chapman, opening up the position for their rookie star.

It seemed there was nothing DiMaggio couldn't do. By July, he'd not only made the All-Star team but was on the cover of *Time* magazine. All of America was talking about him. He finished the season with 206 hits in only 138 games, including 44 doubles, 15 triples, and 29 home runs, for a .323 average. This was particu-

Lefty Gomez (left), always a prankster, checks Joe's tonsils before the start of the 1937 baseball season.

larly impressive because Yankee Stadium was considered deadly for right-hand hitters (the distance to left field was deeper than in any American League ballpark). He also led the league's outfielders with 22 assists, scored 132 runs, and then batted .346 in the World Series against the Giants, which the Yankees won in six games. They were back on top!

The second game of the Series was attended by President Franklin D. Roosevelt. It was played at the Polo Grounds, where the stairs to the clubhouses were located behind center field. The public address announcer instructed all fans and players to remain in place when the game ended so that the President could be escorted out through the centerfield gate in his car.

As it happened, Dimaggio caught the final out deep in center, near the stairs to the clubhouse. For a moment, he thought of running up the stairs, but then he remembered the instructions and remained where he was.

DiMaggio was still there when the President's car approached on its way out of the ballpark. The President turned to DiMaggio and gave him the high sign, an acknowledgment of a game well played, a ball well caught.

When DiMaggio returned home to San Francisco, he was greeted by a brass band at the train station, a parade to City Hall for a welcome-home speech by the mayor, and a crush of children carrying signs and shouting "DiMag Is Back." Joe's proud parents cried tears of joy over the reception. And when Joe used some of his earnings to buy them a new house, even his father had to admit that playing baseball wasn't such a bad job after all!

5

LIFE IN THE BIG LEAGUES

DiMaggio with Lou Gehrig, just after Gehrig removed himself from a Yankee lineup to which he would never return. With Gehrig's illness, DiMaggio became the heart of the team for the remainder of his career.

S ettling into New York was quite an experience for DiMaggio. He was wined and dined in the town's finest restaurants, introduced to the most important people, and recognized by fans wherever he went. Schoolchildren imitated his wide batting stance and short stride, and the nicknames "Yankee Clipper" and "Joltin' Joe" became household words. His salary for 1937 jumped to about $17,000, thanks partly to his oldest brother, Tom, who would serve DiMaggio as a financial advisor for years and years. Most second-year players still earned less than $10,000.

DiMaggio more than earned his salary in '37. There was no "sophomore jinx" or second-year slump for the Yankee Clipper. He led the league with 46 home runs, drove in 167 runners, scored 151 times, and batted .346. On June 13, he hit three homers in one game; on July 9, he did it all, collecting a single, double, triple, and home run in one game. Once again, the Yankees won both the American League pennant and the World Series. Two years in the majors—and two World Series rings for DiMaggio.

But it wasn't just the things he did that made DiMaggio so great: it was often the things he *didn't* do! He was a very smart baserunner who seldom made the common mistake of trying to get an extra base and then being thrown out. Few can ever remember him dropping a fly ball in the outfield, and fewer still ever saw him throw to the wrong base.Without apparent effort, he always seemed to do the right thing. Natural ability, they called it.

Joe's older brother Vince came up to the major leagues in 1937 with the Boston Braves. But Vince was prone to too many strikeouts, which hampered his development, and was never more than just an average player. During the next ten years he would spend time with the Braves, Reds, Pirates, Phillies, and Giants before leaving the game with a lifetime average of .249 and 125 home runs. Unfortunately, it was in the strikeout column that he really stood out, leading the league six times in that department.

Little brother Dominic, however, did better for himself. He joined the Boston Red Sox in 1940 and scored over 100 runs six times, batted over .300 four times, and had a lifetime batting average of .298.

Had he not been overshadowed by his own brother as well as by his teammate, the great Ted Williams, Dom DiMaggio might have been better appreciated. He, too, was an outstanding outfielder, the first to ever record 500 putouts in one season. And whenever his team faced the Yankees, record numbers of DiMaggio fans turned out to see the two brothers square off against each other.

In 1937, DiMaggio bought a restaurant on Fisherman's Wharf in San Francisco and named it Joe DiMaggio's. It soon became one of the most popular places in town. DiMaggio was even voted one of American's "best dressed men" in a magazine article—and with good reason. While most players arrived at the ballpark each day in sports shirts and slacks, DiMaggio always showed up in a suit and tie.

DiMaggio was booed by the fans for the first time in 1938, however. He had begun the season sitting at home in San Francisco, locked in a contract dispute with Yankee management. Baseball fans, many of whom were still out of work and still experiencing the effects of the Depression, were not very sympathetic to DiMaggio's demands. He wanted to be paid almost as much as Lou Gehrig, nearly $40,000. The Yankees felt $25,000 was more realistic, and cer-

DiMaggio duo: in 1941 Boston's Dom DiMaggio (left) played on the American League All-Star team with his brother Joe.

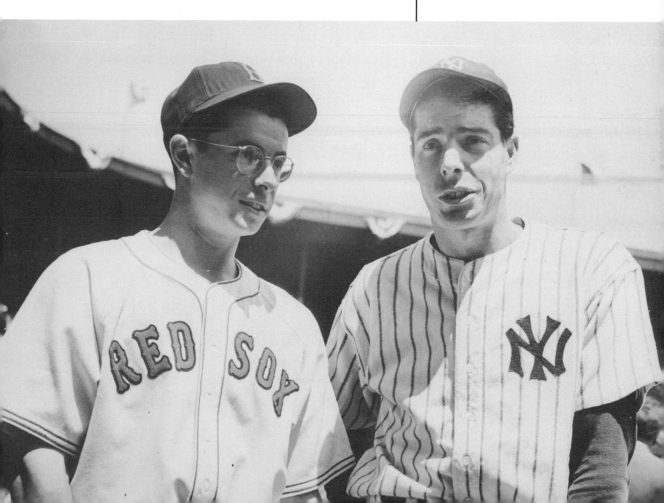

tainly a handsome salary for the time.

As a result, DiMaggio missed all of spring training. By the time he signed and rejoined the team in April, he'd already missed several regular games as well. In his very first game, he collided with Joe Gordon, the team's new second baseman. When Gordon had to be carried off the field on a stretcher, the fans let DiMaggio have it. That was one of the few times they would ever take their frustrations out on him. But it was a valuable experience for DiMaggio. It gave him some small idea of what life was like for most players.

"They pay for their tickets, they have a right to boo," DiMaggio said. It was a good way to handle the incident. Instead of criticizing the fans, he quickly won them over. Soon afterwards, all was forgiven.

The '38 season was not as impressive as 1937 had been, though most players would have been more than satisfied with DiMaggio's .324 average, 32 home runs, and 140 RBI's in 145 games. That this could be considered an off season only showed what grand expectations the fans had for DiMaggio. Still, for the third time in his three seasons with the Yankees, the team won the pennant. And, also for the third time in a row, the Yankees won the World Series. They defeated the Chicago Cubs in four straight.

In 1939, DiMaggio married Dorothy Arnold, an actress he met while appearing briefly in a film called *Manhattan Merry-Go-Round*. While Arnold would present DiMaggio with his only child, a boy named Joe DiMaggio Jr., in October 1941, their marriage was not a happy one. They separated in 1942 and were divorced in 1944. It was typical of DiMaggio that he never discussed his personal life with interviewers, who soon

learned to avoid all personal subjects if they wanted to keep DiMaggio talking.

Even DiMaggio's teammates respected his privacy. The shyness and reserve he'd had as a youngster never really left him. Though he was able to adjust to being a celebrity—he could give a short thank-you speech at a banquet if he received an award, or discuss the prospects for the new season with a radio announcer—he shielded himself and his family from all inquiries into his private life. He spent a lot of time with his teammates, traveling with them around the league by train, but none of them, except Gomez, ever got really close. Only Gomez seemed able to needle DiMaggio and get away with it, and even he knew where to draw the line.

As 1939 approached, fans questioned whether DiMaggio could return to the form of his sensational '37 season. The pressure on him mounted when team captain Lou Gehrig, who had taken the Yankees to great heights, re-

After winning the 1939 Most Valuable Player Award, DiMaggio was honored with a gold watch and a special citation from New York Mayor Fiorello LaGuardia during a game at Yankee Stadium.

moved himself from the lineup after 2,130 consecutive games. A tearful ceremony was held on July 4, and the dying Gehrig never played again. He had been stricken with a disease called ALS, or amyotrophic lateral sclerosis, which came to be known as Lou Gehrig's disease, and the suddenness with which it hit him stunned the nation. In time, it would destroy Gehrig's once mighty body and leave him confined to a wheelchair in his final days.

Out of respect for Gehrig, manager Joe McCarthy said that no one would ever again hold Gehrig's title of Yankee captain. Had McCarthy not declared that, the job would likely have gone to DiMaggio, for now he was clearly the team's leader.

DiMaggio came through for the Yankees with a super '39 season. He batted .381, tops in the American League, and won his first Most Valuable Player Award from the Baseball Writers Association of America. *The Sporting News* se-

In the famous "Lombardi's Snooze" play of the 1939 World Series, Lombardi was knocked out as DiMaggio scored the tying run in the ninth inning of game 4. The Yankees won the game, and the Series, in the tenth inning with three more runs.

lected him as Major League Player of the Year, and once again he led the Yankees to the world championship.

In this World Series against Cincinnati, DiMaggio saved his best moment for the end of the fourth and final game. Trailing 4–2 going into the ninth, the Yankees scored twice with DiMaggio beating a throw home for the tying run. Then, in the top of the tenth, DiMaggio drove in Frank Crosetti with a base hit to make it 5–4. And he came all the way around to score himself when Reds' catcher Ernie Lombardi was knocked over and stunned by Charlie Keller. The play came to be known as Lombardi's Snooze. The Yankees won the game, 7–4, for their fourth world championship in four seasons with DiMaggio.

The record streak of four consecutive world championships came to an end in 1940 with the Yanks finishing third. But DiMaggio continued his winning ways, earning his second batting title with a .352 mark, belting out 31 home runs, and driving in 133.

And then came the golden year of 1941.

THE STREAK!

T he 1941 season saw Ted Williams bat .406 for the Boston Red Sox, the first player in 11 years to reach .400, and the last to this day to accomplish it. Though Williams was to Boston what DiMaggio was to New York, it was typical of the fates and fortunes of their two teams that Williams's biggest year would be overshadowed by DiMaggio's.

On May 15, DiMaggio began a hitting streak that seemingly knew no end. Game after game, he got one or more hits. On and on, the streak built. At first, only the most avid fans were interested. They began talking about his great minor-league streak of 61, but that, after all, had just been in the minors. As DiMaggio's major-league streak lengthened, however, the big national magazines were alerting the public to what was happening. The major-league record was then 44 consecutive games, set by Wee Willie Keeler in 1897. Keeler had been an entirely different type of player, though, a singles hitter who would slap at the balls and simply try to "hit 'em where they ain't." For a hard-hitting slugger like DiMaggio to hit so steadily was another story. But DiMaggio kept his streak going until he passed the Yankee record of 29, Ty Cobb's best showing of 40, and the league record of 42, held by George Sisler.

Fans would huddle by their radios each evening to hear how long DiMaggio could extend his amazing streak. He was the talk of the nation when he finally passed Keeler. Then, every day the streak continued, it was just Joe breaking his own record. A popular song of the day was "Joltin' Joe DiMaggio," and fans were singing, "Joe, Joe DiMaggio, we want you on our side."

The streak went all the way to 56 before DiMaggio and the Yankees faced the Indians in Cleveland on July 17. In Joe's first at-bat, pitcher Al Smith got him to hit a sharp grounder

DiMaggio slides into third on July 15, 1941, the day in which his hitting streak reached 56 games. Two days later, however, third baseman Ken Keltner of Cleveland (# 8) would make two great plays to halt the record-breaking streak.

down the third-base line, and Kenny Keltner made a backhand stab and threw to first for the out. Then, much to the crowd's disappointment, DiMaggio walked in the fourth. Even on the road, most fans rooted for the streak to continue. In the seventh inning DiMaggio belted another shot toward third. Again Keltner handled a tough play and got his man at first.

Jim Bagby Jr. was on the mound when DiMaggio came up in the eighth for what would most likely be his last chance to keep the streak alive. Again DiMaggio hit the ball hard, this time up the middle. Shortstop Lou Boudreau moved' to his left and got a glove on the ball, but it trickled away from him. Quickly, however, he recovered—quickly enough for a double play. Any hope for an extra-inning game and another chance for DiMaggio ended when Yankee reliever Johnny Murphy stopped the Indians in the ninth for a 4–3 win. It was over.

And as though to demonstrate that he was down but not out, DiMaggio came right back to hit in his next 17 straight games, giving him 73 out of 74. Today, you might hear an announcer exclaim over some player who's hit safely in seven of his last eight games. Think about 73 out of 74—when 77 marked an entire half-season! Joe DiMaggio's 56-game hitting streak, now nearly a half-century old, is considered a record that may very well endure forever.

DiMaggio batted .357 for 1941 and won his first RBI championship with 125, despite being sidelined for a month by an ankle injury. Once again, the Yankees won the pennant and this time they beat the Brooklyn Dodgers in the Series to give DiMaggio his fifth world championship in six seasons. Despite Williams's remarkable .406 average, the sportswriters voted

During World War II, DiMaggio played "service ball" in Hawaii with other soldiers. Here he shakes hands with an opposing pitcher named Andy Steinbach in June 1944.

DiMaggio his second MVP award.

Joe Jr. was born just a few days after the World Series. Then, in December, the Japanese bombed Pearl Harbor, Hawaii, and the United States entered World War II. A decision was made to keep major-league baseball going, even though many of its best players would be called into the armed services. Because he was a married man with a child, DiMaggio was not immediately drafted, and was able to play the entire 1942 season. Although he played in every game, he batted only .305 with 21 homers, his lowest totals to date. Then he went home and enlisted in the Air Force.

Military service took three seasons—1943, 1944, 1945—out of DiMaggio's prime. He was

28, 29, and 30 years old at the time, peak years for a ballplayer, and there is no telling what he might have accomplished had he stayed in the game. Ted Williams and Bob Feller were two other great players whose careers were interrupted, but like DiMaggio and hundreds of thousands of others, they went off to do their duty with no complaints.

The Air Force wanted DiMaggio in the United States, playing on camp teams and boosting morale among the troops through baseball. So DiMaggio was fortunate in that he saw no action and suffered no wounds. Even so, he did develop an ulcer and spent time in a military hospital. And when DiMaggio finally rejoined the New York Yankees in 1946, he wasn't the same man who'd left them just three years earlier. And they weren't the same team.

7

THE POST-WAR SEASONS

After the war, DiMaggio found he had three new bosses. Dan Topping, Del Wcbb, and Larry MacPhail had purchased the club while he was gone. There were other changes as well. The end of the war signaled a tremendous interest in baseball by returning servicemen. Attendance figures soared, and the Yankees became the first team to draw 2 million in one season. But by year's end, DiMaggio's only Yankee manager to that point, Joe McCarthy, resigned.

As for DiMaggio, his return to form did not occur quickly. His .290 batting average for the 1946 season was his worst ever, and he failed to drive in 100 runs—another first. Moreover, for only the second time in DiMaggio's career, the Yankees did not win the pennant.

Naturally, there was much talk about whether DiMaggio would ever be the player he'd been before the war. But in 1947 the Yankees won another world championship and DiMaggio looked very much like his old self again, hitting .315, and leading the league in fielding percentage (he made only one error). He also won his third Most Valuable Player Award, this time

The 1949 pennant race between the Yankees and the Red Sox was one of the closest in baseball history, and the teams' two big sluggers were Boston's Ted Williams and New York's Joe DiMaggio.

beating out Ted Williams by a single vote. Williams's lack of popularity with sportswriters was often reflected in these ballots, while DiMaggio always had the respect of the writers and benefited from his fair treatment of them.

Although DiMaggio rarely showed any emotion on the playing field, a memorable exception occurred during the 1947 World Series when he hit a tremendous drive toward the bullpen in deep left center field. As announcer Red Barber put it, outfielder Al Gionfriddo raced "back, back, back, back, back, and oh doctor!" and made a sensational catch to rob DiMaggio of a home run. The newsreel cameras caught DiMaggio disgustedly—and uncharacteristically—kicking the dirt at second base.

It was hard not to forgive the little show of emotion. It symbolized what must have been a tremendous and constant frustration for DiMaggio. He spent his whole career in a ballpark where left center field, his power alley, was known as "Death Valley," and many of his best shots wound up as long outs. Still, there was no place DiMaggio would rather have been—he claimed to have always wanted to be a Yankee.

In 1948, DiMaggio celebrated another sensational season. This time he led the league with 39 homers and 155 RBI's, while batting .320. The next year he was given a raise to $100,000, making him the first player in the league to reach that level.

Prior to the '49 season, the Yankees named Casey Stengel as their new manager. He would be replacing Bucky Harris, who had won in 1947, but not in 1948, when the Yankees finished third. (Much was expected when you managed the Yanks.)

DiMaggio did not say so in public, but his

Brooklyn leftfielder Al Gionfriddo makes a sensational catch against the Dodger bullpen during the 1947 World Series, robbing DiMaggio of an extra-base hit. DiMaggio lost many a home run to the distant field dimensions of Yankee Stadium.

friends knew that he wasn't very happy to have Stengel as a manager. Casey liked to clown around with the press, and that was not the Yankee image DiMaggio had grown up on around McCarthy.

As it happened, however, DiMaggio had bigger problems than a new manager in 1949. Injuries were beginning to take their toll on his athletic body, a sleek 6'2" that usually weighed in at about 195 pounds. An arm injury had made it almost impossible for DiMaggio to throw out runners, and a bone spur in his right foot often caused him great pain. The great DiMaggio was starting to feel the signs of aging that hit many athletes in their mid-30's.

DiMaggio's foot kept him on the sidelines on opening day—and the days that followed. It was a lonely time for DiMaggio. He lived by himself in Manhattan, and without baseball, there was little to occupy him. The pain did not decrease. Even after DiMaggio had an operation, he could only get around on crutches and was unable to go to the ballpark. That would have been frustrating under any circumstances. But DiMaggio felt particularly bad because the Yankees were locked in a tight pennant race with the Red Sox and there was nothing he could do to help them out.

Finally, in late June, just in time for the showdown series with Boston in Fenway Park, he staged his remarkable comeback, pushing the Yankees into first place.

He played in 76 games the rest of the way, hitting .346 with 14 homers and 67 RBI's. He might have done even better, but he was sidelined once more, this time by a virus, near the end of the season. Weak and out of shape, he returned to the lineup for the final two games of the year, again against the Red Sox, but now with the American League pennant on the line.

On the first day, October 1, the Yankees held Joe DiMaggio Day at Yankee Stadium, and nearly 70,000 people turned out to salute their hero. DiMaggio said he wanted to "thank the Good Lord for making me a Yankee," and then he thanked his teammates, calling them "the gamest, fightingest bunch of guys that ever lived."

DiMaggio's return again proved a big lift for the Yankees, who swept the two-game series, won the pennant, and went on to win yet another World Series, besting the Brooklyn Dodgers for the third time.

Still, it was a sad time for DiMaggio. His mother was dying of cancer; his father had passed away in May. And with all his own injuries, perhaps he knew that the end of his career was approaching.

In 1950, however, DiMaggio came back with a .301 season that included 32 home runs and 122 RBI's. But even though the Yankees won the Series again, it wasn't a happy year for him. Manager Casey Stengel had moved DiMaggio from his usual fourth place to fifth in the lineup, and the proud veteran's feelings were hurt.

One bright spot in the season was the All-Star Game, in which DiMaggio made his eleventh appearance. He was a perennial choice for these teams, though oddly enough he rarely shined in them. Altogether, he batted only .225 with one home run in 40 times at bat. In his rookie All-Star Game of 1936, he went 0-for-4 at bat and allowed a low liner off the bat of Gabby Hartnett to get past him and roll to the fence for a triple. And in 1938, he picked up a wild throw made by third baseman Jimmie Foxx on a bunt

In 1951 a rookie named Mickey Mantle (right) joined the Yankees to play right field. But when DiMaggio announced his retirement at the end of the year, Mantle took his position in center. Both are in the Hall of Fame today.

The Yankees retired DiMaggio's uniform number on Opening Day at Yankee Stadium in 1952. Only Babe Ruth's # 3 and Lou Gehrig's # 4 had previously been retired by the team. Here, a representative of the Hall of Fame makes the presentation.

to third by Leo Durocher and fired it over the catcher's head and into the National League dugout. Durocher raced all the way around with a bunt "home run." These moments were not DiMaggio at his best. He seemed to save those for his real team—the Yankees.

The 1951 season brought a new face to the Yankee lineup, a 19-year-old switch-hitter from the cornfields of Oklahoma named Mickey Mantle. Almost at once, writers began calling him "the new DiMaggio," just as 15 years earlier they'd hailed DiMaggio as the "new Ruth." The Yankees themselves saw Mantle as DiMaggio's successor in center field—"some day." For now, however, Mantle was put in right field while DiMaggio continued to patrol center.

DiMaggio missed a lot of games with ailments and injuries in 1951 and wound up with the lowest average of his career, .263. But even so, the Yankees again won the pennant, their tenth in DiMaggio's 13 seasons with the team.

In the World Series against the Giants, DiMaggio drove in five runs in six games and belted his eighth World Series homer. In the last of the eighth inning in the final game at Yankee Stadium, he hit a double. As he stood on second base before some 62,000 New York fans, a tremendous roar burst from the crowd and filtered down to the Yankee Clipper. It was as though many in the ballpark that day sensed they had just seen DiMaggio's last time at bat.

They were right. Not wishing to let his play decline even more, and still gripped by the painful bone spur in his heel, DiMaggio decided to retire at age 37. In just 13 seasons in the major leagues, he had collected 361 home runs. Only four players up to that time—Babe Ruth, Jimmie Foxx, Mel Ott, and Lou Gehrig—had more. Amazingly DiMaggio had struck out only 369 times in his career, just eight more strikeouts than home runs. Most home run hitters today would reach that total in three or four years. And DiMaggio's lifetime batting average was an outstanding .325.

At the press conference announcing his retirement, DiMaggio said, "You all know I've had more than my share of physical injuries and setbacks during my career. In recent years these have been too frequent to laugh off. When baseball is no longer fun, it's no longer a game, and so, I've played my last game."

8

A GENTLEMAN IN RETIREMENT

DiMaggio went home to San Francisco, where he lived with his widowed sister Marie, in the same house he had bought for his parents at the start of his career. The Yankees retired his #5, and offered him a job as a television announcer on pre- and post-game interview shows over the New York station that broadcast their games. DiMaggio agreed to give it a try, but he was still basically shy and felt uncomfortable talking to a television camera. He lasted only one season, 1952.

It was early that same year that DiMaggio was introduced to Marilyn Monroe, one of the most glamorous movie stars Hollywood had ever known. She was as famous in her field as DiMaggio was in his, but she was just approaching her greatest stardom, while DiMaggio had just passed his.

Despite his legendary shyness, DiMaggio began a courtship with Monroe, and it wasn't long before he invited her home to meet his brothers and sisters. Then in 1953, Joe's brother Michael drowned in a tragic fishing accident and Joe turned to Marilyn for comfort. The couple's closeness grew, and they were married in San Francisco on January 14, 1954.

Hollywood's most glamorous movie star, Marilyn Monroe, married DiMaggio at San Francisco's City Hall on January 14, 1954.

The marriage was not a happy one. Some people thought that DiMaggio was jealous of his bride's growing fame and popularity. At one point, after she received a tremendous ovation from servicemen in Korea, she was said to have told DiMaggio, "You never heard such cheering," and he was said to have replied coldly, "Yes, I did."

Whatever the real problems were, no one knew. But in less than one year, DiMaggio moved out of their apartment and they were divorced.

Their marriage may have been short, but their friendship lasted until Monroe's death in 1962. When Joe became a special spring training instructor for the Yankees in 1961, he brought Monroe with him to Florida. Monroe always knew she would count on DiMaggio in times of need, and it was he who arranged for her funeral and made sure that fresh roses were regularly placed on her grave for many years. Curiosity about their relationship always remained high for DiMaggio's and Monroe's millions of fans, but neither one ever publicly discussed it.

In 1955, DiMaggio was elected to the Hall of Fame. But perhaps the greatest honor came in 1969, on baseball's 100th anniversary. To celebrate that milestone, a nationwide vote was taken among fans and sportswriters to choose baseball's "Greatest Living Player," and they picked DiMaggio. That same year, the Yankees dedicated a plaque in his name in center field at Yankee Stadium, alongside the monuments to two other immortals—Babe Ruth and Lou Gehrig.

DiMaggio was always the featured guest at any gathering of old-timers. He played in their games until the early 1970's, when he felt he was embarrassing himself by failing to live up to his young fans' expectations. He did not want to be remembered as an inept old man. He wanted to be

Until illness forced him to miss a Yankee Old Timers Day in 1988, DiMaggio appeared in every one since 1952. He always received a huge ovation, even from fans who had never seen him in his major-league days.

remembered as the graceful, natural athlete he was. His place in history and his image with the fans were very important to him.

In 1968 and 1969, DiMaggio served as a vice-president and coach for the Oakland Athletics, who had just moved to that city from Kansas City. In his new role, he was one of Reggie Jackson's first batting coaches.

DiMaggio's next baseball job didn't come until 1980, when his friend Edward Bennett Williams, a noted Washington lawyer, purchased the Baltimore Orioles and asked DiMaggio to serve on the team's board of directors. In between those two jobs, however, DiMaggio's fame spread to a new generation through the airing of television commercials.

In 1972 he was hired to do commercials in New York for the Bowery Savings Bank, and 17 years later was still going strong in one of the longest advertising relationships ever conceived. Around the same time, he became the national spokesman for Mr. Coffee, a coffee-brewing machine, which made him a familiar visitor—a well-spoken, handsome, distinguished, and sincere gentleman—in millions of American homes.

In 1976, President Gerald Ford presented Joe DiMaggio with America's Medal of Freedom. The Yankee Clipper was a true American hero, whose fame spanned the generations. As Ernest Hemingway, the great American novelist, had once included him in his book *The Old Man and the Sea* ("Have faith in the Yankees my son. Think of the great DiMaggio"), decades later pop musicians Simon and Garfunkel included him in a verse of their hit record "Mrs. Robinson" ("Where have you gone Joe DiMaggio, a nation turns its lonely eyes to you...").

In 1987, DiMaggio underwent surgery to install a pacemaker to correct a faulty heartbeat. He was soon pronounced healthy and returned to his busy schedule of personal appearances. In 1988, President Ronald Reagan invited him to the White House for a state dinner honoring Soviet leader Mikhail Gorbachev. During the evening, DiMaggio called Reagan aside and asked if he could arrange to have the two leaders sign a baseball he'd brought with him. It was a surprising request from one who had given out thousands of autographs over the years. President Reagan accomplished the task, and DiMaggio went home with what was probably the only baseball ever signed by a Russian head of state.

Joe DiMaggio exceeded the world of baseball by bringing honor and respect to himself as a person. He always behaved with dignity and integrity, and never spoke ill of others. A naturally private person, he remained in the public eye long after his playing days were over. But baseball was the arena in which his great fame was earned, and he never wandered far from it. Even in his 70's, he still looks fit in a baseball uniform, and the image of him taking the big stride at bat or roaming the spacious outfield of Yankee Stadium will forever be part of the game's history.

CHRONOLOGY

Nov. 25, 1914	Born in Martinez, California
1931	Quits Galileo High School in tenth grade
1932	Signs minor-league contract with San Francisco Seals
1933	Sets Pacific Coast League record 61-game batting streak
1934	Signs with New York Yankees
1936	Debuts with Yankees, setting rookie records for home runs and RBI's
1939	Wins first MVP Award
Nov. 19, 1939	Marries Dorothy Arnold
May 15, 1941	Begins 56-game hitting streak
July 17, 1941	Streak ends
Oct. 23, 1941	Joe DiMaggio, Jr., is born
1941	Wins second MVP Award
1943–1945	Serves in World War II
1944	Divorces Dorothy Arnold
1947	Wins third MVP Award
1949	Signs first $100,000 contract in American League
Oct. 1, 1949	Joe DiMaggio Day at Yankee Stadium
Dec. 11, 1951	Announces retirement
1952	Does post-game TV shows on WPIX, New York
Jan. 14, 1954	Marries Marilyn Monroe
Oct. 27, 1954	Divorces Marilyn Monroe
1955	Elected to Hall of Fame
1968–1969	Coach and vice-president, Oakland A's
1969	Named "Greatest Living Player"
1976	Receives U.S. Medal of Freedom from President Ford
1980	Named to Baltimore Orioles board of directors
1988	Misses first Yankee Old Timers Day in 36 years

JOSEPH PAUL DI MAGGIO

NEW YORK A.L. 1936 TO 1951

HIT SAFELY IN 56 CONSECUTIVE GAMES
FOR MAJOR LEAGUE RECORD 1941. HIT 2
HOME-RUNS IN ONE INNING 1936. HIT 3
HOME-RUNS IN ONE GAME (3 TIMES). HOLDS
NUMEROUS BATTING RECORDS. PLAYED IN
10 WORLD SERIES (51 GAMES) AND 11 ALL
STAR GAMES. MOST VALUABLE PLAYER
A.L. 1939, 1941, 1947.

MAJOR LEAGUE STATISTICS

NEW YORK YANKEES

YEAR	TEAM	G	AB	R	H	2B	3B	HR	RBI	SB	AVG.
1936	NY A	138	637	132	206	44	15	29	125	4	.323
1937		151	621	151	215	35	15	46	167	3	.346
1938		145	599	129	194	32	13	32	140	6	.324
1939		120	462	108	176	32	6	30	126	3	.381
1940		132	508	93	179	28	9	31	133	1	.352
1941		139	541	122	193	43	11	30	125	4	.357
1942		154	610	123	186	29	13	21	114	4	.305
1946		132	503	81	146	20	8	25	95	1	.290
1947		141	534	97	168	31	10	20	97	3	.315
1948		153	594	110	190	26	11	39	155	1	.320
1949		76	272	58	94	14	6	14	67	0	.346
1950		139	525	114	158	33	10	32	122	0	.301
1951		116	415	72	109	22	4	12	71	0	.263
Total		1,736	6,821	1,390	2,214	389	131	361	1,537	30	.325
World Series (10 years)		51	199	54	6	0	0	8	30	0	.249
All-Star games (11 years)		11	40	7	9	1	0	1	6	1	.225

FURTHER READING

Allen, Maury. *Where Have You Gone Joe DiMaggio?: The Story of America's Last Hero.* New York: E.P. Dutton, 1975.

DeGregorio, George. *Joe DiMaggio—An Informal Biography.* New York: Stein and Day, 1981.

DiMaggio, Joe. *Lucky to Be a Yankee.* New York: Rudolph Field, 1946. Updated, New York: Grosset & Dunlap, 1951.

DiMaggio, Joe. *The DiMaggio Album.* New York: Putnam Publishing, 1989.

Halberstam, David. *Summer of '49.* New York: William Morrow, 1989.

Meany, Tom. *Joseph Paul DiMaggio, the Yankee Clipper.* New York: A.S. Barnes, 1951.

Moore, Jack B. *Joe DiMaggio: Baseball's Yankee Clipper.* Westport, CT: Greenwood Press, 1986.

Silverman, Al. *Joe DiMaggio: The Golden Year, 1941.* Englewood Cliffs, NJ: Prentice-Hall, 1969.

INDEX

MARTY APPEL is the author of 10 books on baseball, including collaborations with Tom Seaver, the late Yankee captain Thurman Munson, and former Baseball Commissioner Bowie Kuhn. His "First Book of Baseball" is one of the top-selling introductory reading books on the sport and a nominee for a Washington Irving Book Award. He is Executive Producer of New York Yankee baseball on WPIX television in New York, and a former Yankee public relations director.

JIM MURRAY, veteran sports columnist of the *Los Angeles Times*, is one of America's most acclaimed writers. He has been named "America's Best Sportswriter" by the National Association of Sportscasters and Sportswriters 14 times, was awarded the Red Smith Award, and was twice winner of the National Headliner Award. In addition, he was awarded the J.G. Taylor Spink Award in 1987 for "meritorious contributions to baseball writing." With this award came his 1988 induction into the National Baseball Hall of Fame in Cooperstown, New York.

EARL WEAVER is the winningest manager in Baltimore Orioles history by a wide margin. He compiled 1,480 victories in his 17 years at the helm. After managing eight different minor league teams, he was given the chance to lead the Orioles in 1968. Under his leadership the Orioles finished lower than second place in the American League East only four times in 17 years. One of only 12 managers in big league history to have managed in four or more World Series, Earl was named Manager of the Year in 1979. The popular Weaver had his number 5 retired in 1982, joining Brooks Robinson, Frank Robinson and Jim Palmer whose numbers were retired previously. Earl Weaver continues his association with the professional baseball scene by writing, broadcasting, and coaching.